Splitting Seeds:

Songs and Stories from the Threshing Floor

Mary Potter

with Marjorie Turner Hollman

Silver Lake Press

ISBN-13 978-0615688015

Mary Ellen Potter and Marjorie Turner Hollman

Splitting Seeds: Songs and Stories from the Threshing Floor
Includes Poems, Illustrations and Memoir

1.Memoir 2. Poetry 3. Clinical Depression 4. Anorexia
5. Christian Inspiration

To My Husband
Paul
My Forever Friend

ACKNOWLEDGMENTS

My husband Paul, my creative children, and my dear granddaughter Kate always inspire me with their love, and enthusiasm for life and laughter. I love you!

There are many family members and friends who have touched my life and given it color and dimension. I give thanks to them for being part of my journey and I am grateful and love you all . . . just for who you are.

My friend Katherine Levin (Katia), my son Erik's Godmother, studied theology at Boston University and took a course with Elie Weisel, author of Night and many other books. He wrote in French and Katia provided English translations for him. She brought him my poems to read. Thank you, Katia, for that gift.

Elie Weisel is completely filled with forgiveness and he has no bitterness in him, even as he has stood strong against what he feels is evil or wrong in the world. He is one of the holiest men I've ever met. I'm grateful for his encouragement to share these poems.

I could never have compiled this book without the loving patience and insight of my dear friend Marjorie Turner Hollman. Her hours of listening to my fragments of thought were like my handing her a few legs and wings, which she then molded into a butterfly.

Marjorie's friends Sue Richardson and Ellen Chagnon contributed invaluable editing assistance. They helped shape the book into its final form, and offered positive suggestions that made the book much better. Bless you!

TABLE OF CONTENTS

Introduction

1. Splitting Seeds
2. Clipped Wings
3. Balloon Song
4. Green Brass Bugle
5. Shining Moments
6. She Laughed
7. Silver Castle
8. Frost Comes so Early
9. Soft Rock
10. Cookies in the Sky
11. The Screaming
12. Daddy Mountain
13. Dancing in your Mindfield
14. Driving the Night Home
15. For Sarah's Graduation
16. The Psalm
17. Reflections
18. The River
19. Fragmented Light
20. Tender Friend
21. You Sing
22. I Hear the Light
23. A Part of Me
24. Blest Be the Tie that Binds
25. Voices
26. The Secret of Flying
27. To Erik
28. Sleeping Rebecca
29. For Adam
30. Wind and Wings
31. Absolution
32. Dry Bones
33. Love Came in a Whisper
34. The Word was There in the Beginning

Afterward

INTRODUCTION

These poems are from half my life ago. The narrative is much more recent, created in partnership with Marjorie Turner Hollman. As I have matured, my life has become full. It's like splitting seeds or a branch that decided to completely strip itself and regrow, attached to the true vine. The poems feel like the skeleton, and now I'm getting to put the flesh on the story. I love the image of the threshing floor, since sometimes you have to get the crap knocked out of you to get to the harvest, which is wholeness.

The narratives follow the poems, and were written thirty years later than the poems, with the perspective that time can provide. Hopefully, the narratives provide some insight into what I felt when I wrote the poems, but more importantly, how I see life now. I hope to be clear that this book is not about blame, regrets or excuses.

I've discovered that you have to bleed into poetry. You have to sit and smell that pain or know that pain to connect to it. Some people would rather have everything simply rhyme and be just fine. But when a poem hits a certain part of someone's heart, a connection is made. If this book helps anyone who is stuck someplace and can't articulate her pain, I'm so glad. Perhaps this book can speak to her and provide some tools for healing.

My youngest son Erik tells me that he has given copies of these poems to many different people he has known. Some people who have read the poems don't understand them. It's OK if this happens; perhaps the poem wasn't meant for them at that time. My hope is that this might be something I can leave as a legacy for anyone who needs it.

Somewhere between the swaddling
and the thorn,
Between the Magic Star and the
Trumpet Morn,
I wander lost....
Weary of the mountain,
Asleep within the valley.

Splitting Seeds

Within my darkness -
This wretched, cold, uncertain stillness,
A choice in tears is made -
I shall be a splitting seed!
Darkness is but fertile earth
In which mind severs from heart
And spirit groans and twists in shreds.
In the coming apart of self,
Torn flesh, tears, blood and soil
Mingle together to herald
One splendid transformation -
Green life pushes forth from shattered shell,
Stretching itself beyond all pain
To greet a tender song that waits
Within the Holy Light of Dawn.

January 13, 1987

1

Splitting Seeds

When I made the first compilation of these poems I chose to end with the poem "Splitting Seeds," because it meant so much to me. Now, as I include narrative with the collection, it seems fitting to *start* with this poem.

At the bottom of the illustration you can see roots, a splitting seed, and out of the seed comes a torrent of different circles that hold fire and a G clef, a star, a dove, and a shooting star. It's a conglomerate of things that have all come out of this split seed.

All the illustrations for this book came later; the poems came first. Over the years my son Erik has encouraged me to write more. My husband Paul asked why I didn't write more poetry, but for now, here's what I have.

I often look at roots and trees and think of healing the branches of our families. Pruning means pain, but by allowing the gardener to do the pruning, joy comes as he removes what is bad, or in the way. The logjams are removed, the life-giving sap flows, and then the fruit comes out.

This poem about the process of coming to life was prophetic. The seed was in the ground, in darkness. It felt itself rip open and didn't understand the process because it had never really seen the light. But in faith it came into being, believed and reached to the light.

This poem really affected me; I felt badly for the seed. In trying to see myself as that seed in the ground when I wrote it, I visualized the light above, and what that seed might be feeling.

As a kid I used to love to stick things in the ground and wait to see what came up. You learn pretty quickly that if you put a rock in the ground, nothing happens; the rock just stays there. And if you bury money, more money won't appear, sad to say! Thinking about this reminds me of Jesus' parable of the talents and the servant who buried his talent. (Matthew 25: 14-30)

You know, some seeds never split open because they prefer to stay in the darkness; it's just too painful for them to rip open. That's the gist of where I was at that time.

Clipped Wings

I clipped my wings one night
Left them neatly in a dream
That I covered over in tears.
Why fly to fall I asked?
Why love – to hurt?
I turned, walking down the mountain,
Vowing to walk the level path
Never looking to the sky.
I had all but forgotten –
Until your wings brushed past me
On a joyful flight to the Sun.
I paused and in pain,
I felt a fluttering call within a long ago
And wept for clouds and starshine.

1981

2

Clipped Wings

The illustration that goes with this poem is of me with broken wings and falling stars. I had almost given up the idea of ever flying, of doing anything. But seeing that other burst of light go by, (in reference to the poem), I felt that I was remembering something good; that perhaps there was still a chance that those wings were going to grow back.

Maybe my wings wouldn't stay clipped; maybe there was a chance for growth. In the midst of the crisis that was my life, somehow I experienced a flash of hope that it wasn't the end of the story. Creating this poem allowed an interjection of hope. The figure in the back of the drawing is perhaps an angel saying, "Come on, Mary, you can do it."

There was a moment in therapy when I said, "This is too hard; I'm not doing it." It reminds me of when I was giving birth to Erik, who was nine pounds, four ounces, in a posterior presentation. Admittedly, after the fourth kid you'll push out a mule if you have to, but I can still see myself sitting up in bed and announcing, "I'm just not going to do this." It was the most ridiculous thing for me to say, since he was right there, ready to be borne. My doctor said, "Come on, Mary, I know you can do it. Come on." Grudgingly, I agreed. "Oh, all right." One more push, and he was out.

I know that in therapy there was a point when I thought, I'm taking my toys and going home. And someone said to me, "It's just another inch." Somehow, it helped, and I didn't give up.

Balloon Song

1. I let go of my balloon too soon
   and it flew away.
Hope it landed on the moon!
My playmates sang, 'till the lunch bell rang
   then they went their way,
But still today, I hum the tune.

Refrain:
I'll live to be a hundred anyway,
Born fresh and new the start of every day.
My secret? It's very plain-
I feed the child and starve the pain,
But my friend, why does it seem
You feed the pain and starve your dream?

2. The child inside had to run and hide
   when the taxman came,
Collecting all his don'ts and dues.
My dog didn't bite, I was polite,
As I played his game,
And gave the dreams I wouldn't use.

3. Toys in the box, the cradle rocks,
   and my teddy bear smiles,
Sorting secrets he's been told.
My head's in a race for a quiet place,
I can go for awhile,
To let my daydreams all unfold.

(cont.)

4. I stood in the shade to watch the parade,
as the clown tumbled by.
He seemed to call my soul by name.
As we stood face to face,
I noticed a trace of my tears in his eyes,
At least our colors ran the same.

Look! There's my balloon.
It's softly landing
on
the
moon!

1982

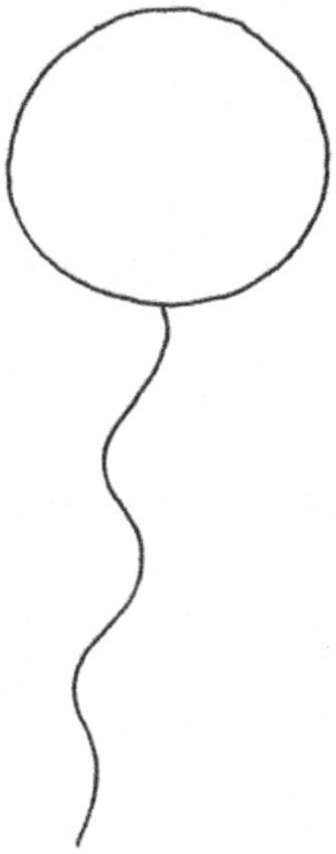

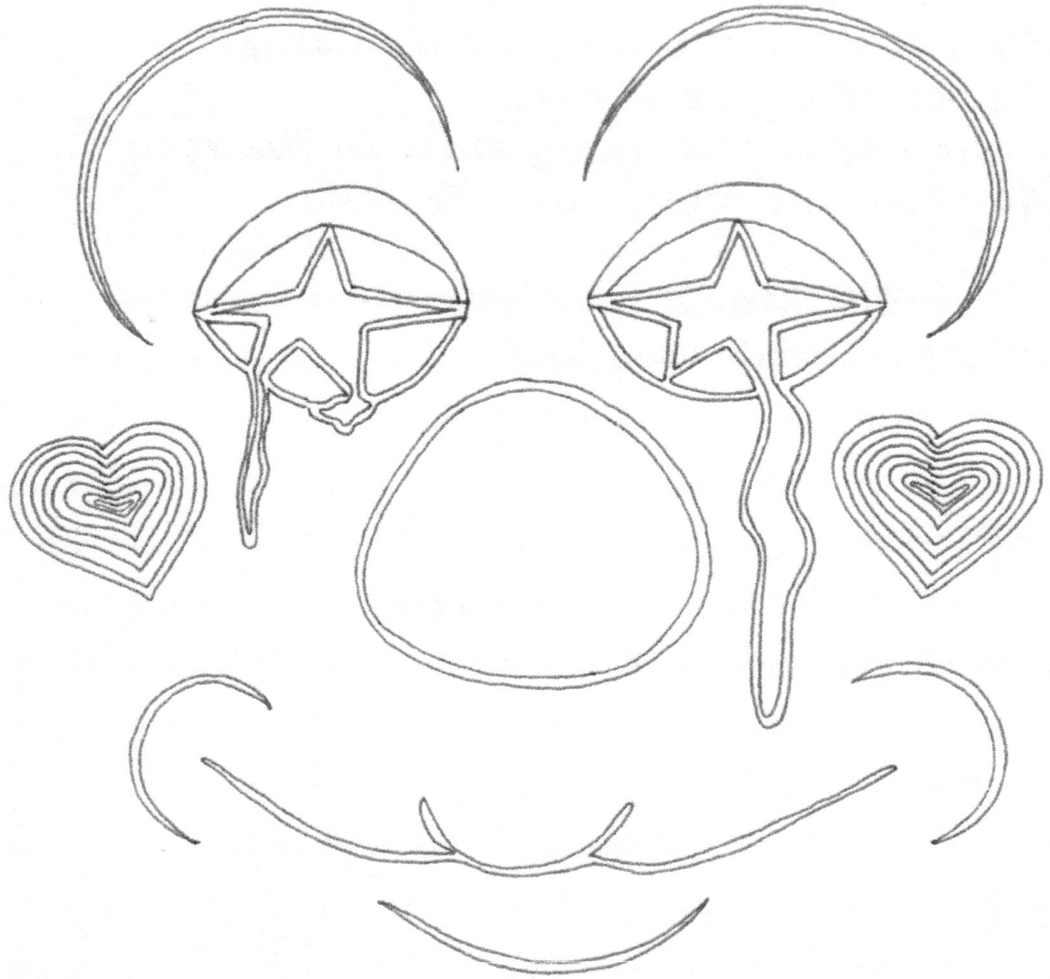

3

Balloon Song

I barely remember making these drawings, but I tried to make them as simple and stark as I could, because I was living in a world of black and white. I used to sing this as a song, accompanied by my guitar, but I don't remember the tune.

It was very difficult for the therapists to get past my sense of humor. I was able to use humor in a good way to empower other people or myself. But I also used it to hide real feelings; it's a double-edged sword. I'm getting better with this, and I'm also getting better about recognizing this in other people when I talk with them. When I see others using humor to mask pain, I call them on it. "I know what you're doing..."

I was ultra polite when I was growing up; it was something I used it as a coping mechanism. I said to people in so many words, "I'll give you whatever blood and bone you want, but I won't give you my major organs; I'm keeping enough to survive." But there were things I shouldn't have given away. These ideas all began to merge in the poem when it talks about the "toys in the box and the cradle rocks."

I began to understand a lot of things, because of my children. I was able to begin to reflect on what I did as a child and what happened to me. I was determined not to pass on those things to my children.

When the poem talks about watching the parade, the clown is me in the way my life was then. You know, as long as you dress nice and keep clean and are the perfect little girl and are funny, everything appears to be fine. But you can see the tears in the clown's eyes, even when he's smiling.

The balloon at the end of the poem represents hope. My children loved the story of The Red Balloon, how a child chased the red balloon. I believe that a lot of people let go of their balloons too soon. Hold onto that balloon as long as you can; enjoy that moment.

At the end of the poem the balloon softly lands on the moon: it didn't drop into the ocean and choke a dolphin. My dreams went some place safe—to the moon or perhaps into the arms of God—until I was able to use them again. But those dreams were filled with more than helium; they were filled with hope. And now they are filled with good things. They aren't lost; they aren't going to fly away.

Green Brass Bugle

The green brass bugle noise,
Of rusty treasures and earthly toys,
So drowns the pure gold of His voice,
(My cluttered soul cannot rejoice.)

The weight of earth - cold iron bars -
My feet in mud - heart in clouds,
As petty self in darkness shrouds,
The wings that ache to kiss the stars.

Damn the pride!
Bless the desolation,
That drives me to His side,
In tearful expectation,
Of His still voice - pure solace
freedom bright!
The shining song that slays the night.

One price for peace, dear Love has willed,
All voices but His own be stilled.
Yet in this stillness ever blessed,
I find faint memory of the rest.

1982

4

Green Brass Bugle

As I've revisited these poems, it's been cathartic for me to read them out loud. There is a façade that we put out there to hide all the ugly things we feel inside. But we end up with tarnished and broken things, the nice brass bugle and the band. That band drowns out the pure gold of God's voice. Our souls can't rejoice because we're so busy putting up that false storefront where we tell people that everything's great. But if you don't dismantle the storefront, it's going to come down on its own.

Inside, behind the façade, there are some really yucky messes, broken things. What I understand now about, "Damn the pride, bless the desolation," is that pride keeps us from calling out and admitting that, "It's not all that great in here." Another line in the poem says, "One price for peace, dear Love has willed, that all voices but his own be stilled." It's pride that keeps us from asking for help.

When I was six or seven, I had a wretched stomach bug. One of our neighbors, the sweetest lady you'd ever meet, came over to see how I was doing. She walked in and there I was with a bleached out face, afghan wrapped around me, the bucket waiting for the next time I threw up. Mrs. Johnson looked at me and said, "Oh, Mary Ellen, how are you darling?" I was taught to always say, "I'm fine, thank you, and how are you?" so I parroted, "Fine thank you Mrs. Johnson, and how are you?" She shook her head and smiled so kindly at me. "Oh, no darlin', you're not fine. You're very sick." I insisted, "I'm OK, really."

I grew up with this attitude, but what God really wants is for us to run to His side. He says, "I'll get rid of all that stuff that's holding you back." He just wants us to let Him hold us, to be real. This doesn't mean that you have to be whiney. Oh, I hate whining. Complain, sincerely expecting that the Lord is going to hear and help, but don't whine because it's so annoying.

Erik, my son, was two when he got the idea that he was God. He told my husband Paul, who said, "No Erik, you're not God." So he came to me, screaming and whining. He stomped his little feet and said, "Daddy's mean!" "Why's Daddy mean Erik?" I asked. "Daddy says I'm not God and I really am." I was trying to cook dinner and had little patience for this. I looked at him and said, "Honey, you're not God. Do you know why you're not God? Because God doesn't whine." He ran out of the room crying, but I had to tell him the truth: God doesn't whine.

Erik, now twenty-seven years old, is very close to his God. I'm constantly amazed at his faith. Perhaps God was so close to that little boy that they were "one" in that moment and that was the only way he could articulate it.

Shining Moments

Sometimes our lives seem so cruelly
misaligned,
Spinning out of control past each other
Chased by ghosts of future and past.
Yet, there is a rare, shining moment
Into which two souls fall headlong.
Their thoughts and dreams dance
together, stripped and bathed
in light,
Blessed by a holy knowing.
Two souls bonded by this special moment
Never cleanly break away—
Scattered pieces of each other graft on
and weave into the rest of their days
Composing one glorious and eternal song!

1983

5

Shining Moments

I wrote this poem thinking of people I've made soul connections with; even when those connections have been for just a brief period of time. In the course of our flight, our journey, everything drops away and there is a holy space, a holy time when souls connect and rejoice without fear. In time the connection will break away, but there will always be scattered pieces of each other grafted onto and woven into one another.

Working on this book together with Marjorie has created a soul connection, with her and with anyone who reads this. I become part of your story, you become part of mine, but we're not knotted together. Rather, we're woven together in a pattern; God's pattern. It's what he has done to bring our lives together in a holy moment.

There's an instant of truth when two souls are willing to stand together and be honest and true with one another, no matter how painful that is. How precious. It will never be lost, but each of us is also free enough to float away to go do whatever we next have to do.

She Laughed

She laughed~
  as her flesh fell down around her
  like a threadbare coat
    well worn, past mending
  For a brighter Star she was befriending,
  Leaping bare and brilliant
        into the Light.

Old loves wept~
  as they patched with tears
  their fresh-torn seams,
  They looked for traces in their dreams,
  Of bits of light that
        held her smile.

She laughs~
  as she spins and dances free in flight
  and finds within this Star
    her forgotten wings
  With a thousand senses of Heavenly things
  She once lost in her first lullaby.

1·19·84

6

She Laughed

I've learned to become friends with poems, because they are living entities. I recall writing this poem spontaneously in about five minutes after a friend died of breast cancer. I've come to realize that it relates to myself as well as to other people. The illustration is of a woman stripped bare, dancing in the fire.

When my children were growing up I tried to explain death to them. I told them, "It's like having a wonderful coat, or clothes that you really love, this wonderful set of comfortable work clothes that God put on you. They've served you well, but people's clothes get a little worn. Sometimes you can put a patch on them, sometimes they have to be sewn in places, but there comes a time when they are no longer of service. You have to lose them, and God gives you a new set of clothing. He clothes you in His love and His peace. He clothes the real part of you, and you can let those old clothes go."

After we're born and our mothers start singing and talking to us, it's easy to forget the angel voices that we were so attuned to before we were born. When a person dies, she is able to laugh and hear those voices again, and say, "I'm free; I don't need this coat that I tried so hard to mend and patch. Now I can let go and have this beautiful new body." But the people you've left behind cry, because they can't see this.

Silver Castle

I built a silver castle on
what I thought was a solid dream
Yet it was shifting sand-
I dressed a corpse in a satin coat-
I heard the stench
I smelled the scream
As the castle fell by its lifeless hand.
My castle- so real and glorious!
Even her flags struggled to dance in the wind
as they fell
and fell.
On a cold rock I sit-
with yesterday's rags
and tomorrow's crown,
Sounding the trumpet in the rain,
"Build again!"
"Build again!"

2-19-85

7

Silver Castle

My senses were so mixed up when this poem was created that I used to tell my doctors I could taste my pain and smell different things. But despite this, there was always a thread of hope. The picture is a sad lady with a crown and tattered robes, sitting on what looks like the ruin of a castle. She has a trumpet in her hand.

Even though I felt so disconnected—my mind, heart and spirit—I felt God holding me somehow, keeping me together. I used to say, "I don't know where you are God, but you know where I am because I'm not like car keys. I may lose my car keys but you don't lose people. Even if I don't know where you are, at least you know where I am." That's what held me together through some really bad times.

As this poem came into being, I had the hope of being able to rebuild something. We often have a lot of dreams and expectations that are built on shifting sand, rather than built on the Rock.

What we build on the Rock lasts. To that I say, Amen.

Frost Comes So Early

Refrain
Almighty take the brokenhearted,
Almighty take the broken,
Almighty take the brokenhearted,
Rock them into one, my Lord.

1. Brown baby cries for bread, my Lord
Sweet Chariot don't swing low,
Heavenly shoes too long coming,
And Frost comes so early in the morning.

2. Earth child standing at the river, my Lord
His dreams are troubled in the water,
Trees are falling like tears around,
And Frost comes so early in the morning.

3. Widow sitting by the window, my Lord
Memories rolling down her face,
Kettle's crying tea for one,
And Frost comes so early in the morning.

4. Grace come for who don't deserve, Lord.
Hope puts wings on the dream,
Salvation clothes the naked Spirit,
And Frost comes so early in the morning.

11-85

8

Frost Comes so Early

This was written as a song. The illustration shows three bare trees with a single leaf drifting down, suspended in the air. Using chords I composed, I sang this, and accompanied myself with my guitar. It's almost in the style of a spiritual, but with more of an Appalachian feel to it, a very simple folk thing. "Grace, come for those who don't deserve it."

It's always been my dream that people might feel the warmth of God's embrace and be rocked in his arms. I see so much fragmentation and brokenness in people. But God can take each of us and create a tapestry from our broken pieces.

I was looking for that for myself. I was also responding to the pain of all the other people who were with me in the institution, all who were suffering in the world.

I don't know what other people's sufferings are, so I can't add much more than that, but the poem describes many different kinds of sadness that God want to heal us from. The refrain starts the song, and goes between each verse.

Soft Rock

I am a Soft Rock,
a Pliable Wire,
Talk of the Flock,
a Flexible Flyer.
I'm Cool with the River
Hot with the Fire.
I don't burn
I don't burn
I don't burn.

I am a Star Stroller,
a Rainbow Slider,
Deep Soul Troller,
a Sweet Dream Glider.
I'm a Joyful Runner,
a Peaceful Rider.
Home where I am
Home where I am
Home where I am.

Stood tall while I knelt to reach the Sun.
Fire and Ice will not melt if molded into One.
Only circles spin,
Spheres roll.
To the end, begin again,
Learn the tides within the soul.

2·86

9

Soft Rock

One of the things I've struggled with in getting better is that I've often used my imagination, especially my sense of humor, as a protective tool. God intended our imagination to be used as a gift, but we can use it for or against ourselves, and it can prevent us from getting the help we need.

Since my mind has quieted down I'm able to use my imagination in positive ways. This is not to make light of hard things, or to gloss over the pain; rather, to interject hope. Empowering others gives me a little boost of hope so I can reach toward a higher level, a clearer understanding of my own feelings.

If you're going to give your feelings to God, you can't keep them all covered up. I've watched the tools other people try to use: alcohol, drugs, prescribed or not, to relieve or mask the depression or cover it up. Others throw themselves into activities they shouldn't be in. Good or bad, over-involvement in certain projects can end up being an effort to run from life.

I can't tell a person where she's supposed to be. She can only find that out for herself if she stands still. Just for a moment, stand quietly and say, "This is where I'm supposed to be right now." It's important: own it and discover that it's good to have positive things to do.

I call this one of my slightly sarcastic poems. I tried to stay sarcastic, but spiritual, which is kind of an oxymoron; but then again, I love that word.

Cookies in the Sky

Sometimes I think of you and I,
Baking cookies in the sky,
Sipping cups of colored rain,
Wrapping stars in cellophane,
Our pockets are filling.
Such a heavenly appetite,
We'll eat the moon bite by bite,
Fingers sticky with the light,
Where the dreams are spilling.

The milky way is melting, friend,
Into a chocolate covered song.
Somethings cooking at the rainbow's end.
Grab a spoon and come along.

Sometimes I think of you and I,
Baking cookies in the sky,
Stirring sunshine in a pail,
Icing for a comet's tail.
A sunset filled with dishes.
So easy to lose control,
When its time to lick the bowl,
Frosting prints upon the soul,
Tummies fat with wishes.

4·86

For Stephanie, Adam, Rebecca and Erik

10

Cookies in the Sky

My children were quite small when I wrote most of these poems. When I went to Westwood Lodge to be hospitalized, I had to stop nursing my youngest, Erik. He learned to walk while I was away from home. This illustration is an outline of my four children. That's how Steph wore her hair. That's Adam, and then Becky, who always wore a little ponytail with the bow. The little baby at the end is Erik holding a spoon, and there's a dripping star that looks like a comet with a comet tail. This was our fun poem, and is dedicated to Stephy, Adam, Rebecca and Erik, April 1986

My imagination kept me alive during my childhood because there I could be in a different family, a different place and a different time, so I didn't have to experience what I was going through. I got a lot from my Dad, who was very imaginative, very loving and very sweet, which was such a gift.

When I was in the hospital, people asked what they could do for me and I always said, "Take care of my children." That was the most important thing to me. There were so many loving people who stepped in and my husband Paul was wonderful, but some people did extremely special things for my children.

I was in the hospital again when Erik was three or four and Erik's Godmother, Katia, my dear friend, took him with her to Brandeis, where she was getting her doctorate. One of the professors, Mr. Shulkin, gave him cookies when he came with Katia. Erik often talked about "Mr. Shulkin who gives me cookies," (and still refers to him this way even now.)

When Erik went to Brandeis as a student himself, he was sad because "Mr. Shulkin who gives me cookies" had retired, but Mr. Shulkin did want to send cookies for Erik's first day. These thoughts make me tear up because the only thing I could give my children then was dreams. The dreams didn't make sense to the world, but my children could grasp them and hold onto something beautiful.

God did grant beautiful things for my children. They're extremely articulate, bright and creative. That was what I wanted for them, even though I could only give them dreams.

These days, my granddaughter Kate loves to play imaginary games with me. Kate calls me "Nani." She sits in my lap and we make imaginary milkshakes with all the neat ingredients a three-year-old (or a sixty-one year old grandmother) needs.

Sometimes "Nani" is a "blender" for our milk shake games, and I jiggle her until all our ingredients are mixed up just right. Other times I pretend to be an oven and make her into my "cake." I poke her tummy to check if the cake is done. My dad played these kinds of games with me when I was a little girl.

Some nights being an imaginary kitchen appliance to amuse my little Sweet Pea gets very tiring, but the smile stays on my face for days. I know that the games I played with my Dad as a child kept me sane and alive. I played in the same way with my children. Now Kate reminds me again of that blessing.

The Screaming

There is a Screaming in me...
More ancient than my birth cry
Haunting, Howling, yet Heavenly,
Buried alive--
Muffled by the flesh of my daily duty.
Desperate light struggling-
A candle burns beneath the musty rubble.
There is a Screaming in me...
An angry tide confined,
A storm in chains forged of wind and rock.
Waves of despair... and delight?
Sprays of Joy above the struggle,
As shorelight strokes the trembling water.
There is a Screaming in me...
Hungry for a trumpet, strings or clay,
A glowing circle to be born into,
Spun and woven into a peaceful garden melody.
Clumsy fingers dipped in tears,
Trace masterpieces across the empty air,
That vanish as castles stolen by the sea.
There is a Screaming in me...
Like sand and salt it works within the wounds,
Burning, Breaking... Baptizing-
Humbling, Holding... Healing-
With thunder it cries,
"I AM YOUR ALPHA AND YOUR OMEGA!"
The shroud is rent as a splitting seed.

(cont.)

Life flows forth with Light -
A River Released -
As stars, sky and creation applaud
Welcoming their own...
A Screaming with new wings
is born into Eternal Song.

Feb-April 3 - 86

11

The Screaming

In my heart I know why I wrote this poem, but I couldn't articulate it at the time. My doctors often said to me, "You're always smiling and cheerful but we know that you are deeply, incredibly suicidal." I told them that I wouldn't do anything to myself because I didn't want to leave that legacy to my children. I wanted to stay alive for them and for my husband Paul.

This was written during a bad time in my life. When my daughter Stephanie was seven, she came to see me at the hospital. Paul was carrying the baby and she asked, "Mommy, did I make you sick?" I drew her close to me and said, "No, you and your brothers and sister and Daddy are all the reasons I want to be well. You're the reason I want to be whole." In retrospect, I know now that I was "standing in the gap," but I was not going to let this happen to my children. I didn't ever want them to feel guilty or to hand on what was handed down to me.

As I went back to my room that day after they left, I thanked God and said, "Thank you that I could remind her of that, that she and her brothers and sister and Paul are the most precious things in my life. If it wasn't for them I would have taken my life because I couldn't stand to be here anymore."

I knew I had to stay alive and be as well as I could possibly be and reach even above the level the world might set for me. This was for my children's sakes—and to give them something to talk about with their psychiatrists—a joke my friend Katia and I shared. I wanted them to know that I did love them, even though Mommy was a little screwy at the time, because I had lost fifty pounds from not eating and had almost died.

I was determined to hold this pain for as long as I needed to, to heal it, so I didn't pass it on to my children. It felt dangerous, but I felt like I was containing it. God was speaking in it, even though I could feel the screaming, the pain that had to get out, but God was in there with me. I tried to yell louder than the pain so I could hear it. That's how I felt, even as it was so scary.

I wrote this while I was in the hospital. I was trying to articulate what I was feeling inside, and it came to me like an avalanche of thought. It's kind of a difficult one.

To My Darling Husband...

They're climbing Daddy Mountain-
Foot and hand, chin and knee
Safe and warm on Daddy Mountain
Room for tiny climbers three
Sister, Brother, Baby fair
Take their hearts and travel there.
They poke the mountain - and he wriggles
As down the slopes the echo giggles.
With every bounce he softly groans
The victim of their tiny bones.
At once a growl! A warning frown!
Peace is won! They settle down.
I love you, Daddy, kind and sweet
Lined with my babies head to feet!

June 1983
For Father's Day

12

Daddy Mountain

I wrote this for my kids. This was before my youngest, Erik, was born. The other three kids used to climb all over Paul, who was Daddy Mountain.

The idea of the poem probably began as I lay on the sofa watching Paul trying to take a nap on the floor. The kids liked to climb on him when he was on the floor. He sometimes worked the evening shift, getting home at eleven, so he was often tired and tried to grab a little sleep whenever he could.

As I watched them, I got such a kick out of them climbing all over him. Their little feet stepped on places that probably weren't real comfortable, but he was so gentle. They were so sweet and contented with him.

Paul was the next-to-the-youngest in his family; he played a lot with his nieces and nephews. He's always been good with children, but then, he's really a big kid himself—a huge kid.

This was written for Father's Day, before I went in the hospital for the first time. I love this poem.

Dancing in Your Mindfield

Dancing in your mindfield,
A perilous pirouette.
Dangerous, but yet,
The music is so inviting,
glorious, exciting,
I can go on and on!

Dancing in your mindfield,
The Lord only knows,
I've lost a few toes,
But the dance is so sweet
with or without feet,
I can go on and on!

Dancing in your mindfield,
It's really no surprise,
When I close my eyes,
There's starsamid the flames
and they all have names!
I can go on and on!

4·86

13

Dancing in Your Mindfield

This poem is kind of funny but kind of sad. It takes me back to a Han Christian Anderson fairy tale my father used to read to me, about the little girl with red shoes. I used to say to my doctors, "Please, kindly woodsman, cut off my feet because I can't stop dancing."

The dancing was the dance I had to do to please everybody else. I was dancing in a minefield where I shouldn't have been anyway. I was losing my feet and toes but I kept going because I couldn't stop. I don't go into that field anymore; I go to much better fields now, thank you, Jesus.

At this same time I also wrote a graphic novel that isn't included in this book. I tried to use every word imaginable for anger. The character in the story got more and more angry and the words got bigger and bigger until the character nearly exploded.

At the time I wrote the graphic novel I thought, hey, that's pretty funny—but it wasn't funny—it was very sad. I see it now as a tool that the Heavenly Father gave me, but I didn't understand how to use it at the time. I compare it to giving a Skilsaw to a four-year old. Ask her to build a shed in a weekend and you know that someone's going to lose a finger, and you're not getting that shed.

Even when I wrote the most angry and sarcastic of my poems, I always felt a little tap on my shoulder. I sensed that it was God saying, "Don't give up. Don't give up."

I'm able to spot self-destructive behavior in others, and I try to say, "Long-term—it doesn't work. Find other ways to channel your pain." Even if you have just one mustard seed of hope, hold on to it, because some day it's going to be one big, big tree.

Driving the Night Home

Well, Hip Hip Hooray
Here comes the Day
They're Shouting,
"Glory Hallelujah to the Sun!"
But the dusk is coming,
The crowd is running,
Fading away one by one.
Nodding off to Sleep,
Empty promises to keep,
Another party's waiting
on the phone.
I'm out of Luck...
Looks like I'm stuck
Driving the night home alone.

5-86

14

Driving the Night Home (Alone)

I wrote this at a time when I felt that people didn't understand what I was going through. They nodded like they understood, but I still had to go to sleep alone with the darkness.

At the end of the day, you do go to sleep with yourself, even if you're sleeping with your husband or whomever you're sleeping with—you're sleeping with your own soul. This life is still yours, and you still own the consequences of what happens.

I felt like I was going to sleep with darkness, that I was driving the night home alone. I really wasn't though; Jesus was there with me.

A lot of people don't feel that, and I understand. Many times *I* didn't feel it. That's what faith is though; believing what you don't see, what you don't feel. Like we say in the Nicene Creed: "I believe in . . . all things seen and unseen." Sometimes we really have to believe the unseen to discern that it's true, that God is with us.

At the time I felt that everybody else was fine, doing their thing, and there I was, going to sleep still depressed, and I didn't like it. Whine, whine, whine. Ah, caught myself whining! But I don't do that anymore.

For Sarah's Graduation ...
May 1986

Sarah,
You are the waves
flowing blue green, alive -
Laughter and tears,
embracing,
bending,
dancing.
Sisters of the Tide
Content and free.

You are Woman and Child
an innocent sage,
Born Yesterday,
Alive Forever.
A gypsy Pilgrim on a
Joyful Journey.

Go run with your dreams
Embrace the Stars!
Your gentle heart has much
room for Love!

15

For Sarah's Graduation

This was for Sarah, my friend Annie's daughter, when she graduated from college at Oberlin. It was my gift to her for her graduation, in May, 1986. This number of years later, she's still a sweet person.

A Psalm

O Lord, Be My Shepherd
I want so much!
I long to sleep in green pastures.
You show me still waters in my dreams
and I thirst
to be restored.
Your righteous paths by grace I'd walk
and call your Name
Yet I walk in shadows of dust and bones
that draw me backward to the light
There is no fear...
You know where I am
I have hope...
You set a feast of love abundantly before me
amid the barreness of my heart...
I am too overwhelmed to eat.
My head is anointed with tears
My cup, inverted, empty
the river still flows past.
Surely Your Goodness and Mercy must
search for me??
There is an empty room in Your House
Furnished simply by Your Grace where
I would dwell forever.

6·16·86

"A Psalm"

This was my take on the 23rd Psalm. The illustration contains mountains and streams, and a woman with an inverted cup. At the time I wrote this and created the drawing, I was 5'7" and 105 pounds. The doctors told me I had a different kind of anorexia, since I just wouldn't eat. I didn't make myself throw up; I was simply very restrictive about anything that went into my body. After my heart almost stopped, I got pumped full of potassium, and I rewrote this Psalm in "anorexia speak." It's one of my dark ones.

Life is strange. Now that I cannot physically eat without great difficulty because of Multiple Sclerosis (MS), I see this poem in a different way. At that time I had the opportunity to eat anything and chose not to because I was denying myself.

The effects of MS have made eating difficult and time-demanding for me, but I know that food is OK. I eat food that I wouldn't have eaten when I was hospitalized. If the muscles in my throat were frozen then as they are now, I'd have thought that was just great. I don't welcome this now, so I just put some more potato flakes in the soup, or more chicken in the tortellini so I can slide that down.

I've learned the meaning of food, and also of spiritual food. Food is intended to nourish our bodies and spiritual food is truly necessary to nourish our souls.

My difficulty in eating is no longer a tool of destruction; it's a tool that God is using so I can be introspective and more accepting of spiritual food. When I take the Eucharist now, I think, "Wow, now I'm going to eat!" I know that I'm being fed—a real banquet indeed.

I see losing control of my throat muscles as a terrible thing, part of the road I'm walking, but in place of whatever I can't eat physically, God is filling me up with blessings. Like "Cookies in the Sky," my tummy is fat with wishes and blessings. I'm more spiritually full than when I was skinny and refused to eat.

There are a lot of people who stuff themselves with food and starve themselves of graces, blessings and insights. My cup is no longer inverted, however; it's open—my arms are open. My head is no longer down either; it's up. Food is just food, not a source of punishment or pleasure. I feel, despite life's circumstances, that I'm at the banquet table of the Lord.

Reflections

Reflections of a mirror?
Sharp images of glass & paint
Unmoving, without warmth,
Jagged, piercing, shattering to touch.
Reflections in the river?
Wavy images of light and life,
Changing, Flowing, Inclusive
Nurturing, Healing, Gentle to the touch.
A hand brushes across the water,
The rippling reply -
"I feel, I hear."
One affects the other
The hand stirs the stillness
The water stirs the heart within -
Rhythm.

6·19·86

17

Reflections

Mirrors are deceptive, reversing images and deceiving the eye. Some of us put up mirrors while at other times we see through clear glass or through water. I already have trouble keeping my right and left straight. If you put me in front of a mirror I get completely confused!

The accompanying illustration looks like a wavy line with a star. There are two hands merging and their forefingers are merging into the star, touching one another. I think all of these poems are about seeing things more clearly, and connecting in a real way with people.

The River

The river has been chasing me,
Since I dried myself from Mother's womb.
Elusion, Illusion, the mountain
havens were too high
For shelter from that stubborn tide.
I memorized every mountain rock–
One stumble I would die–
The air was too thin to breathe,
There was no green in rocks and sand
to fill my soul.
Then... That Strange Star...
One day it caught me unaware.
So bright, dazzling it blinded me
into Greater Sight.
I fell into the river...
It was warm and wet
Cleansing...
The waves cradled me
Rocked me...
It was my own tears.

7.5.86

18

The River

I think the river that I write about was all my pent up tears and feelings. I was afraid of that river. Once I fell into the river, however, it was cleansing, almost baptizing. Being able to fall into my tears and own them and know it's all right to cry—that's a good thing. Recently I watched my son hold my granddaughter, just hold her, and I cried. As I cried, I thought, I like this; this is a good cry. It feels good. I get excited now, because I know that some cries feel good.

When I was growing up, I wasn't allowed to cry at home. I could cry around my dad, but if I cried around my mother, I was punished or banished, sometimes for a couple of days.

My dad's mother died when he was two days old. His mother was very young, just nineteen, and his father was twenty—they were just kids themselves. Dad was left to die at the hospital; they said he wouldn't take any formula. His grandfather, Carl, my great-grandfather, intended to leave him there, but Carl had a housekeeper who had raised all of his kids, Mary Ellen Webster. When she saw that no one wanted the baby, she marched down to Norwood Hospital and demanded the baby. She carried Dad home under her arm like a little football and got him to eat by putting a little brandy in his milk.

This angel raised Dad until he was eight years old, when she died. But before her death she urged her sixteen-year-old daughter, Auntie Bea, to take care of him, which she did, because Carl's second wife didn't want Bobby, my dad.

Mary Ellen made sure Bobby had special things. She really spoiled him. He told us stories of how much he adored Mary Ellen, and how she and others always looked out for him. I asked Dad once if he felt angry that he'd lived with so many grandparents in so many different places. He said, "No, because everywhere I went somebody loved me. I always felt that, so there was no need to be angry with anybody." It was a wonderful lesson for me. I thought that if my dad could forgive that, then forgiveness must be a wonderful thing.

This was a gift that he passed on to me. I think it enabled him to be an incredible father, and he was. He got up in the middle of the night when my mother pretended she was asleep. He fed us and loved us. I was attached to his hip most of the time and mimicked what he did, sitting and crossing my arms the same way as he did.

When I was older, he told me, "If Mary Ellen Webster had lived, she'd be your grandmother, because that was the mother I knew. I heard stories about my mother, that she was beautiful, but Mary Ellen Webster loved me." So I was named Mary Ellen, after her. She saw a child in need and decided that she was going to have him, and that was that.

In the illustration the lady is dancing in a tempest of fire or water. There's a star and a continual circle. She seems to be happy. As I created the drawing I tried to make sure that there was a continuous line going round and round.

Fragmented Light

My circle spins a fragmented light.
Beams shatter - overlap -
My pain illumines the way
For the sunrise birth of joy.

Your eyes shine - wide open
Brave windows cannot,
will not squint.
Reflect the rainbow back,
Bend tender the spectrums of color.
Stand still sweet artist, friend -
Witness the first wingspread of
a Star.

7·2·86

19

Fragmented Light

I wrote this for a person who was trying to help me at the time. This friend wanted to be open, and attempted to understand what I was trying to say and I appreciated it. I was so fragmented at the time. She wasn't able to understand, but she was OK with that.

It's not possible to get the whole picture when someone's disturbed and in the situation I was in. But the fact that she was willing to look into my heart, my eyes—it was like she moved into my soul.

I wanted to thank her for trying, and to let her know that it was OK that everything wasn't fixed. I felt like I was trying to say, "I've brought you this toy to be fixed and it might still clunk when I pull the string but at least you tried, you were there, and you were open."

This is a poem of gratitude. I encounter so many people who run away from a person who is in pain. Perhaps they're afraid that pain is contagious.

In my mother's day, people never said the word, "cancer," they always whispered it, fearing it was some form of contagion. I see this even more with spiritual or mental illnesses; people are terrified that it's going to stick, like invisible mud.

It's better in that case if you leave the plate of brownies at the door, ring the doorbell and run. I was grateful for those people too. If that's all they could do—to leave brownies for my kids—that's all right. But just being there is the best gift, even if we don't know the right thing to do or say.

Just being there is the best gift anyone can give.

Tender Friend

To Annie

Tender friend-
The sunshine bursts from those tiny holes
you choose not to fill with fear's dark putty.

I never wanted to pierce-
draw blood.
I never wanted to bruise or crack.
My sunlight wanted to dance with you.
My circle spun with yours and blew the pain
away.
The music filled the empty chill with
promise and peace.
We are all held together with holes and
cracks.
Smoothness is only claimed by the Divine
Heart.

Grooved, bumpy, holes, mountains, valleys-
Aren't we the shape of earth itself?
Don't we orbit the one Great Sun?

Tender friend-
Your light warms me.
Your valleys hold my tears.
Your mountains give me hope
I love you!

7.4.86

20

Tender Friend

This poem was for Annie. Her daughter was Sarah, the young girl for whom I wrote the poem for her graduation. Annie died of cancer about eight years ago. Years before she came to visit me a lot when I was hospitalized.

Annie was very cerebral. She was also very musical and very bright. She was my daughter Rebecca's godmother.

I was able to be with Annie at her death. She was in a nursing home nearby, and I was able to help her and relate to her on the level where she was at that particular time. We'd disconnected for years, but as she lay dying we connected again. The scattered things between us came full circle. I know that she was with God and that it was OK, and that her daughter was OK too.

The illustration is an outline of Annie. It makes me smile when I see this image of her.

You sing~
Seemingly unaware of
Someone walking there inside.
A kingly presence with majestic stride,
Moves with passion thru your story.
Harmonious with love's shining glory,
He cuts and heals between the notes.
In awe, I wonder,
Do you feel the thunder
Or are you just at peace
Being one with the song?

For Ann's Birthday
April 14th 1983

January~April 1983

You Sing

This poem was also for Annie, who had a beautiful voice. She played the organ at the church I attended.

She took over the compilation of Erik Routley's "Rejoice in the Lord" Hymnal, which was published in 1985, after he died. Annie readied it for publication, and I was able to help her with the task of correlating the notes and hand printing out the words under the music for each hymn. What an awesome hymnal; it's very user-friendly and accessible.

When I wrote this poem about how Annie sang, she didn't really understand it, but I did, since it was really about me. I just didn't realize it at the time.

I Hear the Light

I hear the Light sometimes -
Chimes begging for a breeze.
Darkness is a chore to swallow
all at once.
I hear the Light sometimes -
Unborn child in dark warm water
Turns a trusting ear for the
sweet thunder of a Heartbeat -
A rhythm of Love,
Music without words.
I hear the Light sometimes...
and wait patiently for Dawn.

7·21·86

I Hear the Light

When I was in the middle of the complete darkness of depression or a bad situation, it was like chimes that stood still. I remember the line coming up for me: "It's very dark in here, but I hear the light." At the time I thought, That's pretty strange.

You know, you have to cling to the light, even though the light doesn't have a sound. After I got out of the hospital, I started hitting myself and scratching myself, since the doctors weren't doing a very good job of noticing that they were dredging up things they were not equipped to deal with. I believe that basically I was struggling with spiritual problems, and the medical doctors weren't able to help with that.

Once a week I try to go through the scriptures about Christ's *Passion* (the events leading up to his death on the cross.) When it comes to the part where he's flogged, I think about the fact that he's taken all of that for us. We don't have to flog ourselves since he's taken that on in his perfect flesh. We've been redeemed, so it's almost an insult to the sacrifice of Christ to injure ourselves. Because we carry Christ within us, we need to be more loving to the temple, which is our bodies, and I believe that by His stripes I am healed. If you have pain, offer it to the Lord. Having him bear it with you is different than making designs on your arm.

The drawing has chimes and four stars, probably representing my kids at the time. The poem says a lot about hope and when life is very, very dark. I used to cling to this poem a lot. I probably wrote it when I was still hospitalized.

There are times now when I can feel God saying, “That’s too painful and unless it’s keeping you from what you’re supposed to do now, you don’t have to remember it. You only have to recall the things that are necessary to be healed and walk forward.” At those times, Jesus goes back with me, absorbs the pain, and frees me to go on.

A Part of Me

There is a part of me
that wants to die
As much as a part of me
that wants to live.
Rock myself on a bed of nails-
Cradle myself in flames-
I yearn to be acknowledged
as I disappear.
Safe in starvation~
Denied, Damned, Desperate...

7·23·86

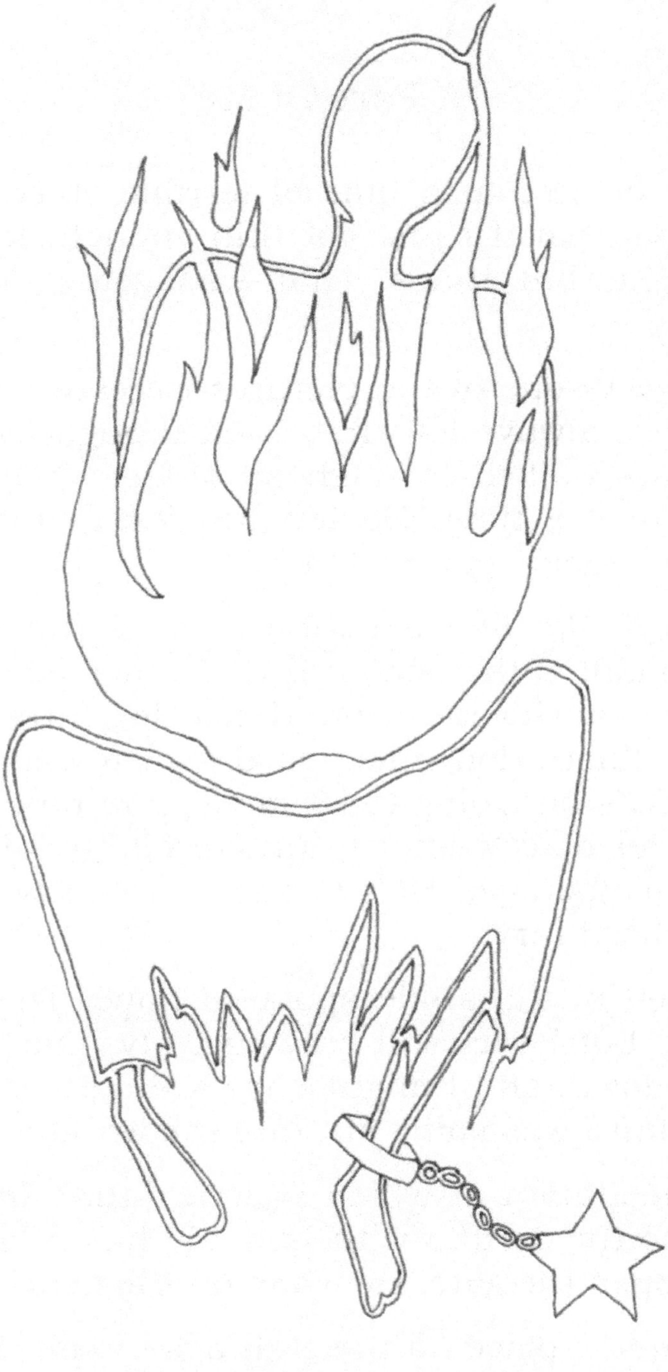

23

A Part Of Me

This poem was created at a time of terrible starvation. I thought that I could disappear if I just got thin enough. It wasn't a clear, cognitive thought, but that's what was going on and I fought against it.

I had hope in every one of the pictures I created. I'm still hooked on to that hope. I always felt that, even though I felt pretty awful right then. Jesus walked through all of this with me, but I was unaware of it at the time. He left his testimony through these poems, and the poems kept me here.

The illustration looks like a cauldron, and there's a person in flames. The top half of the person is disconnected from the bottom half, and there's a shackle around one leg, attached to a star. Looking at the illustration now, I'm drawn to the foot chained to the star. The star's not going to let me go and now I know who the Star is. No matter how much I think I'm disconnected, I know I'm not going to be consumed. He's not going to allow that to happen, no matter how hard I try.

The star chained to the ankle spoke of hope. The poem perhaps feels desperate, but I was still crawling. My nails might be really thin and worn down, and I might have to take a breath, stop, and close my eyes, but I was going out into the world again.

I made up a meditation in which I picture that Jesus has invited me to come into the garden with him. He has a beautiful garden, but only I can open the gate. He waits on the bench in the garden.

Before I can enter, I place all these things—I call them the broken toys of life—into the bag and toss the bag over my shoulder.

That long walk into the garden is hard because my bag is so heavy, with all those "toys" in my pack. But how wonderful to see Jesus sitting in the garden with his arms open, and hear him say, "Sit down, let's see what you've got. Let's see what we can fix, and what you're willing to take out of the bag and give to me." One by one we take things out. There are some things I want to keep in the bottom of the bag, maybe because I'm too ashamed, or it feels too scary to take them out.

It is a delight to see Jesus take things out, fix them, put them together, or put light into them, using his heavenly duct tape, which is his mercy, forgiveness and incredible insight. One by one, those "toys" get fixed, and then I simply leave them there with him. Once my bag is empty, I'm able to crawl in his lap and go to sleep.

There's a hymn, "I come to the garden alone," which I have always loved. As he was praying, C. Austin Miles, the author, had a vision. He saw Mary Magdelyn in the garden after the crucifixion, mistaking Jesus for the gardener. At the end of the hymn, she doesn't want to leave, but "He bids me go through the voice of woe, His voice to me is calling."

These meditations have been a really helpful healing tool for me as my mind has gradually quieted down. I've found that some people are too frightened to turn the spotlight on those rat sounds in their minds. But they're really just tiny little bugs with big feet and Jesus can squish them so easily.

Blest be the Tie That Binds

"Blest be the tie that binds..."
Hands clasped without white knuckles,
The thread unbreakable joins the hearts.
No need to fear in parting
The ties are long...

Binding –
 Not Bondage.
I would bless such tender chains
With just the weight to hold
 my course in flight.
To fly –
Yet not be blown away!

"Blest be the tie that binds..."
Woven lives
 of hope and pain
 colors muted humble
 vibrant bold
The Tapestry of Love!

6·19-20·86

Blest Be the Tie that Binds

I want to be bound to someone in Christian love, charity and truth. Having a rope with a chain and hook to bind someone is not in God's plan. Being connected in a spiritual way with each other is to be bound together as we were intended to be.

In the illustration there are clasped hands, kind of a border around that looks like contour lines, or corn rows around it. These must be the ties that bind.

When I was five, I was hospitalized over Christmas. A man came into my room after dark dressed as Santa Claus. I was scared to death of anyone who wore a mask, but this was Santa Claus! I was very sick and Santa came in and said, "Hello, sweetheart. Merry Christmas." He then tucked a little doll under each of my arms and again said, "Merry Christmas." His memory continues to bless me.

My mother insisted that I leave one of the dolls at the hospital. She said there was some little girl at the hospital who needed it more than I did. I cried and cried since I didn't want to leave her.

It was like having twins and abandoning one of them. Being made to share like this was a trigger for me needing to be the "perfect girl." My mother was trying to teach me how not to be selfish, but it was the wrong lesson at the wrong time.

My Dad used to love to tell me stories his grandfather had told him, and funny adventures with his friend John Maloney, who was "afraid of nothin'." These tales told us, "Don't be stupid." Yet I also heard, "Believe in your plans." Dad told these crazy stories in such a funny way, but John Maloney was a wonderful guy; he died in WWII. John and my Dad were like brothers to each other.

They lived in the same household for years. Bea Webster (Mary Ellen Webster's daughter,) who raised my Dad after Mary Ellen died, worked for the Maloney family, and she and my dad lived with the Maloney's.

When I was hospitalized as an adult, the counselors brought my parents and my husband Paul to talk with me. This was for me to tell my mother painful things I needed to say. They had to drag the words out of me because I didn't want to hurt her, but I had to do it. Mom denied everything, so I cried, then Mom cried.

My father said, "Honey can I ask you something?" I said through tears, "Sure, Dad," and he said, "Well, when you were a teenager and you were kind of clutzy and, I love you, but you fell down a lot." Then he said, "One evening you hopped around and slammed into a wall, and I laughed, even though I didn't mean to." I looked at him, baffled.

Then he said, "I laughed at you. I felt really bad afterwards because I shouldn't have laughed. Is that why you're in the hospital?" I told him, "Dad, I don't even remember doing that," and I started to laugh, so he said, "Oh, OK then." My father was always able to make me laugh.

Later, my Dad drove me to counseling appointments, and often asked if he had "done this" to me. A wise counselor told me to tell him that he was the reason I'd survived. I think of him as the angel that God sent.

Mama Syl (Sylvia), my mother's best friend, was my other angel besides Dad. She gave me all the hugs and loves my mother wasn't able to give. Sylvia never had her own children but loved everybody else's. She came; she saw; she helped. That's what they put on her holy card after she died. She raised other people's children and went wherever she was needed.

Now that Mom's died, she understands. I feel Mum, Dad and Sylvia praying for, and encouraging me.

Voices

Voices have hands that are seldom empty,
Brandishing swords or spheres of light.
Some wounding, yet wounded,
Some wounded, but healing,
All walk in and out of rhythm
across the listening heart.
Some tear thru tender flesh as
twisting steel without a soul,
Yet some rock the restless Child
with sweet silent Lullaby.
Thoughtless, joyous, tender, cruel...
Eternal echoes joined hand in hand,
Form the circle where spins our
deepest dreams.

8-12-86

Voices

This poem is helpful for people who have voices from their past that they listen to. I believe that the human voice and the voice of the dark one can cut deeper and cause more wounds and more blood than any sword fashioned by man. The poem probably came to me in five minutes when I was sitting alone in my room at the hospital; an avalanche of words.

I was thinking about how hurtful words can be. You know the adage, that I'd rather you beat me than use those words on me. The scars heal from those beatings, but the words and the way they are said seem to settle so deeply into people's hearts.

I wrote this poem for myself, but I also wrote it for the other people who were hospitalized there with me. They seemed to be suffering not so much from physical trauma as from passive-aggressive verbal abuse—such haunting experiences.

Now I'm able to see that one word or phrase can be really powerful, something a person can hold onto, even if it's just to say, "Jesus, Jesus, Jesus, help me," over and over again. It's something to hold on to.

We sometimes use words in our brokenness to break other people. Some words tell a person that she's no good and not worth anything; this can absolutely cut the legs off a person's soul.

I learned the difference between how our words compare with the Divine Word, which is always truth, healing and positive. If we allow God, and listen to God, we can use words to help and heal people.

The Secret of Flying

The secret of flying is not at all
in the art of self-navigation,
But rather the degree to which you befriend
the Ways of the Wind.
You must stand bare and burden-free,
Perched on the edge of your dreams and reality
And fall totally into the elements.

In this free flight
With the pain and passion intertwined.
Do not consider too highly your wings,
Thank the Wind who bears them!
Neither give glory to the brightness
of your own thought
Praise the Sun who lights your path!

Quiet the self-sung melody of your flight
And set your heart to the Sky Master's Music.
With Sun, Wind, Go Homebound in Harmony,
Losing yourself within His Wings.

1983

The Secret of Flying

This is about being willing to stand on the edge; about having the confidence to go into freefall. All of us get to a point in our lives when the only thing we can do is to release and freefall. It's the hardest thing to do, especially if you have control issues, or fear issues, or any other issue at all.

There are camps you can go to where they say, "Fall and don't look back." But everyone always looks back to make sure it's the substantial hunky person, not the scrawny one, who's going to catch you.

I love the saying, "You can never fall farther than your knees." God's going to catch you, but you have to be willing to let go of whatever it is that is holding you back. Those things that hold you back, those false senses of security have to be released.

Flying is about being able to open your arms, no matter how scared you are. Take a deep breath and fall, knowing that God is going to catch you. It takes a lot of practice; flying practice.

That's what I was feeling when I wrote this poem. Don't go looking for your wings. Stop checking the wind gauge to decide if it's the right time. Enough worrying about whether you've found a good landing pattern, or whether the engine is all set. It has to be total trust at that moment, and if you can do it, or even get close to doing it, the end result will be incredible blessing.

Even if you get banged up a little, He mends you, because you're willing to trust, which is what God asks of us. It's taken me years to learn to trust in God, not people. People, even those who love you, are going to fail you; it's part of our nature.

This poem is dedicated to my eldest daughter Stephanie. We found a book of names before she was born and learned that Stephanie meant garland. We said, "That's perfect, Stephanie Joy, because she's the crown of joy of our marriage." She's always lived up to her name.

I'm so proud of how willing she is to dive into life with such enthusiasm. She is a professional photographer and has a keen eye and sense for detail. She is always "camera-ready," prepared to hurl herself, body and soul, into finding that perfect shot.

Photography is an adventure for Stephanie, and listening to the stories behind her photos is so much fun. She definitely flies into her free falls and looks forward to each new adventure.

Erik~

You stood alone today
With no support except
a sticky smile-
One step-wobble-two steps.
I knew you did it before
but we pretended it was
a first.
I clapped inside and out.
~Joy and sadness~

7.25.86

Sleeping Rebecca

Where are you now, sleepy one?

Do you tease the limbs of trees
Swinging in the breeze
of an endless spring?

Do you fly, clouds and stars
chasing by
Sailing on a lullaby
Dancing to an angel's song?

Could you stop awhile,
behind that smile
free of guile,
To weave me into your dreams?

1982

To my son, Adam on his fifteenth
birthday...

I've watched you grow it seems
in no time at all but,
When you love a child....
Time flies beyond measuring...

I remember your first kick,
a flutter... a definite kick...
A father's hand against a little foot
unborn!

Now I look up to see you..
You kick with legs longer than
I could dream of!
Almost a man...
Yet I remember the firsts....
the milestones and
rejoice!
I look forward to living my life
with you always in it!

Love,
Mom

March 26th 1995

27, 28, 29

To Erik
Sleeping Rebecca
For Adam

These poems are about my three younger children.

My son had turned a year old that April and I wrote "To Erik" in July while I was in the hospital. He was crawling when I left, and was able to walk when I returned home.

My family didn't want me to know that he could already walk, since I'd missed his first steps. Whenever they came to visit me they sat Erik down rather than stand him up to help him walk. One day they called him over and he stood up and walked over to me. Everyone said, "Oh, look, he's walking!" I knew they had tried to save it as a surprise for me and I thought it was sweet, since they were thinking of me. I saw him walk, which was a happy time, but it also made me extremely sad since I'd left him as a baby and came back home to find a toddler there, in the space of two months.

When Erik went to Brandeis for college, I was able to walk the hills of the Brandeis campus with him. I'd been walking with a cane for nine years prior to that time, but was granted a fourteen-month remission from MS. I had the sense that God was holding me in His hand. My older son Adam was deployed overseas with the Marines at this same time. I was able to walk the campus with Erik, and when Adam returned home safely I ran into his arms as he got off the airplane.

There are so many special things about Erik: his birth, his life—his three siblings are drawn to him. He has a gentle spirit.

Becky was so little —just a baby—eight months old, when I wrote "Sleeping Rebecca." One day she was sleeping in my arms and I started wondering what she was thinking. It was a happy time and the other kids were playing.

When I read this poem it brings to mind the feeling I now have with my granddaughter Kate. When she's sleepy, she takes my thumb and likes me to rub her nose, because that's what she does with her Mommy.

You wonder what a child is thinking in these peaceful, beautiful times. Now that all my kids are adults, I miss when I could hold them in my arms and keep them safe.

My father taught my son Adam how to stab crab apples onto sticks and fling them. Adam flung lots of those apples, but one day when I came home from work I noticed that one window was shinier than when I left it. The kids had had to call Ba (my Dad) to come repair the glass because Adam had flung a crab apple through the living room window.

I wrote the poem, "For Adam," when he was fifteen. I watched him grow, stretch and try his wings. He was going to do this, invent that. He had big dreams, a little like John Maloney—it was kind of scary.

It seems like God has always given me extra-special wrapped, beautiful presents in these joyful moments. He may take some away because it's necessary in the whole scheme of things, but He still throws in surprises.

All my kids make me smile. I wouldn't trade them for anyone!

These poems about my children make me feel hopeful. There are still a lot more wonderful things God's going to let me see my kids do. That's His grace.

Wind and Wings

The breeze from your wings
stirs a storm in me.
Sweet wind, a morning reverie
sounding, "Come to Life!"
A welcome tempest framed in
rainbow ~
Dancing flames rock in the sea
From which a song wet with
birth arises,
"Praise wind and wings, fire
and friendship
unconsumed!"

10·21·86

Wind and Wings

This poem was the celebration of a friendship. My friend Annie took me to Bermuda as a treat after I got home from the hospital. It was a beautiful time and a nice gift from Annie. She footed the bill and wanted me to enjoy that freedom. It was almost too traumatizing for me to go, however. I felt like I had to make the bed and sign out, like when I'd been in the hospital.

When they put a chocolate on my pillow I freaked out since I just wasn't used to it. I was accustomed to a regimented, institutional life. After having lived such a restricted life and landing in Shangri-La, I felt like I was still in jail, just a prettier jail. Still, it was a gift I continue to treasure.

Absolution

Soul Scouring
To the bitter bone – atone.
Overpowering is
My need to fly whole.
Blood Letting,
In the bleeding - needing
But never getting
Absolution for my soul.

Accuser, accused
I cast the stone ~ alone
Embracing Pain, confused
I cut my heart on broken wings.
Where... what is grace?
Purging for peace ~ release,
From a dark empty place
Where only a nightmare sings.

11·21-22·86

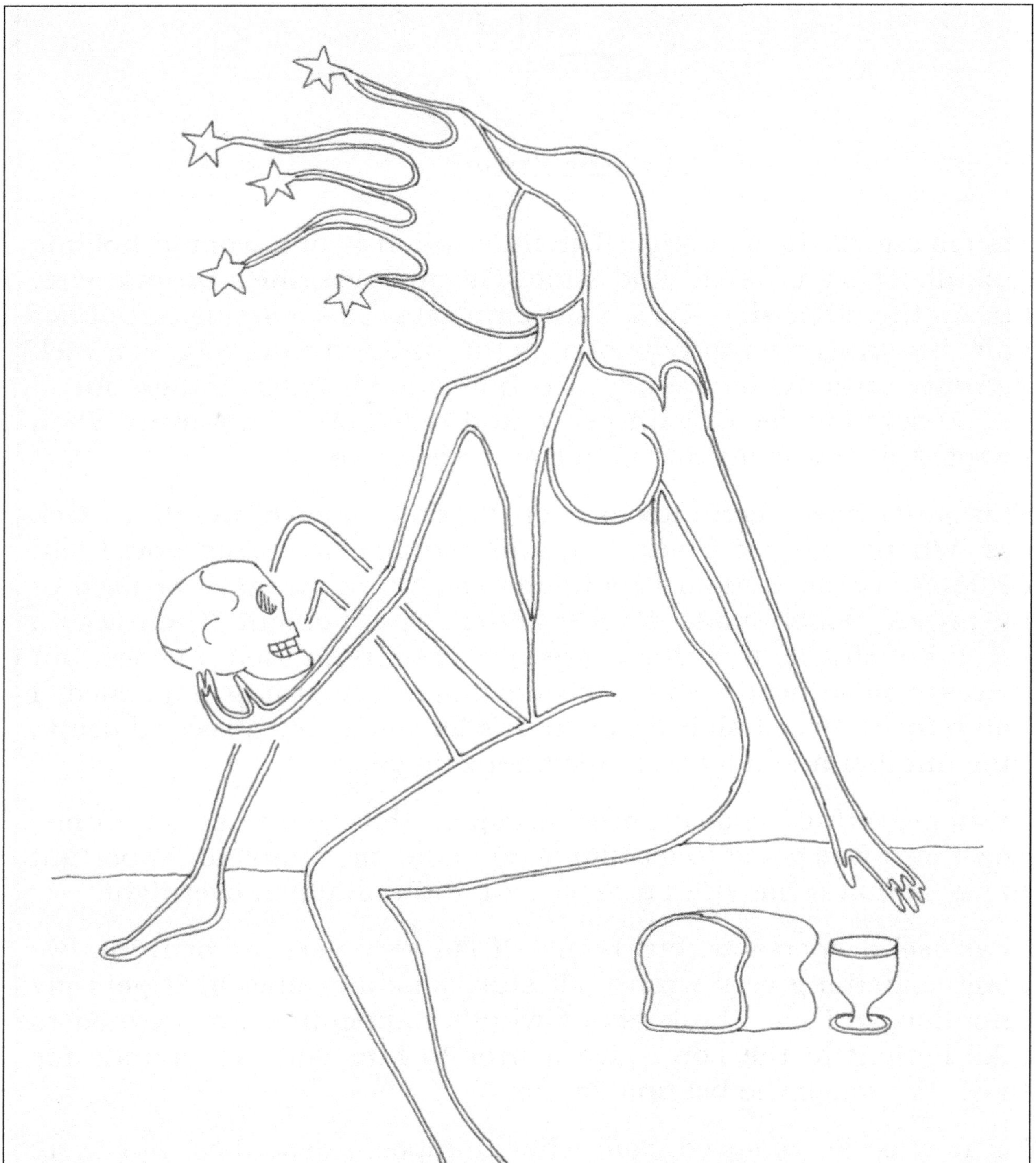

31

Absolution

This is one of the sad ones. The illustration is of a woman holding a skull. There is bread and wine. On one side she's normal size, but on the other side she's a skeleton. Stars are coming out of her hair. It's an oxymoron type of a picture. I was trying to give myself my own absolution, literally scrubbing the terrible things out of me. Absolution comes with peace and redemption, however. When I wrote this, I was my own judge and executioner.

This must have been after one of the times I gave myself a black eye. Whenever I got frustrated, and couldn't articulate how I felt, couldn't cry, or thought I had done something wrong, I bruised or hit myself, which made me feel better for a moment. There was a second of shame, then there was a release, then I felt a peace, but it was a false peace, since the next time something happened, I had to hurt myself all over again. It's like going for a second drink, then another and another—anesthetizing yourself.

I was prayerfully healed once I accepted that God really loved me, and that I was going to let him in to make me complete. Important to say is that it has been a process: it didn't happen overnight.

I can feel deeper now, but better. If I'm very nervous or think I've done something very wrong, I'll start pinching myself. It gets my attention so I can think about what's happening. I've learned to take it right to the Lord, give it over to him and he reminds me that, "I've taken the beating for you."

I'm now so far removed from what this poem describes, but there are people who still do this, and my heart breaks for them. I understand that need to be totally scrubbed clean before you can live or feel.

I now have the tools and I have the Master of the tools walking with me to help me. I still fall down, but He fell three times and He got up and helps me. I can "get" the gospel now. Beyond the darkness, He's right there, so I can get through it. I don't have to go run and fix it myself. He will help me and guide me to wherever I am supposed to go.

It's a process, and it's still happening, and will continue to happen until they close the lid on me. I'm in such an incredibly better place now. I know that the more you walk on the journey, the more stones you encounter and that more hurts are going to come up.

I don't want to make light of any of this. There were people hospitalized at the same time as I was who didn't make it; they killed themselves. I know that God was there even in that last moment, that He took their hand, because there's always that last moment: He's the master of time.

In "Absolution," the first line tells it all.

Dry Bones

Why does the skeleton always smile,
Stripped bare of flesh and soul?
An empty temple devoid of
praise and song.
It stares without eyes...
Mocking me.
~ The only voice-
Bones clacking on Bones,
Dancing in the first
chill of Autumn.
Perhaps it has nothing left but
the absurd Truth,
That I've been too full to comprehend...
Them bones..
Them bones...
Them dry, dry bones...
Now hear the Voice of the Lord!

Dec. 1-13, 86

Dry Bones

It was Halloween when I wrote this next poem. As I wrote, I thought about the skeletons at Halloween time blowing in the wind. I was so empty, but was so full of pain. The fullness was the pain, so I kept trying to empty myself—to disappear.

This is one of my depressive-state poems, and yet there was always hope, at least there always has been for me. There's that song, "Sometimes I feel like a motherless child..." What I love about the original version is that it continues, "But then I get down on my knees and I pray." It's one of my favorite hymns. So there's the hope, and people tend to leave that other part off. I get down on my knees and pray. Then I'm filled up again.

My poems always have a light sense, a wry sense of anger, maybe pain, but there's always a little bit of light interjected. And the title was very appropriate for me, since I was very skinny at the time.

Love came in a whisper
Soft as the Virgin Child's lullaby
Sung to her treasure born to die
For other mothers' sons.

Love came in a whisper
As Simeon's dream was fullfilled
By a babe whose course had been willed
To carry the world upon His heart.

Love came in a whisper~
At Calvary's Tree sins chains
were broken
As tender words of truth
were spoken
By that Virgin's Child who rose
to life.

Love comes as a whisper
To waiting hearts in earth's
despair
Who look to meet Him in the air
As silent Love turns to a Shout.

Christmas Eve -
1982

Love Came in a Whisper

This is a poem I wrote for Christmas Eve in 1982. It was way before I became aware of my depression and the things I was dealing with. At the time I felt very hopeful.

The Word was there at the Beginning,
Profound Truth, Solemn, Brilliant, Sweet
Jesus came to set it to music
Then the Word could dance - it was complete.

Seeds of our dreams embrace the new day
Bursting with brightness into flower
The Saviour's blood, as nuturing rain
Gives sinners hope and heaven power.

Lord give your spirit to bless our words
Wings to lift our dreams, new seeds to sow
Set our hearts to Your ryhme and music
Love's Symphony in our lives to know.

May '83

The Word was There at the Beginning

I think of the first chapter of the Gospel of John when I read this poem. You know, "The Word was there at the beginning." John 1: 1-5 *(New Revised Standard Version)* tells it all.

"In the beginning was the Word, and the Word was with God, and the Word was God. He was in the beginning with God. All things came into being through him, and without him not one thing came into being. What has come into being in him was life, and the life was the light of all people. The light shines in the darkness, and the darkness did not overcome it."

Amen.

A Final Word from Mary

Most of the poems included here were written during, before, or soon after my hospitalizations for anorexia and severe depression, now thirty years ago. I was writing from my soul, rather than with my brain. Sometimes I didn't quite understand what I was writing, but it made sense to my heart.

Do I still have battles with depression? Yes, in the sense that because of the disease of MS, which I have, one of the primary things people complain about is fatigue, and it affects your mind. Dirty tricks can come in and fool you, so I sometimes question myself, wondering, "Why can't I do that?"

Despite these challenges, I try not to let my spirit be drained. I allow my body to rest, and try to keep from being spiritually drained or I'll get into more problems. It's been a process through the 1980's, and the 1990's. I'm 61 now, and the work is ongoing. My whole life has been a process, like those cathedrals that take a hundred years to build, but then you can look around and say, "Wow!"

My dad liked to say that Michelangelo could have finished the Sistine Chapel much quicker if he had used a paint roller. Healings are the same way: it's a lifetime process with no shortcuts.

I do believe in instantaneous healings, but to think that after a person is a walking basket case, that all of a sudden she's going to be "all set," is just not how life works.

Healing from anorexia is a lifetime process, a process of vigilance. There are people who have died from the disorder: I almost died when my heartbeat became so irregular. Food was a frightening thing for me; part of me was trying to disappear to escape my pain. Even so, I was trying very hard to eat, for the sake of my kids and my husband.

Well, I'm still here, and food is no longer frightening to me—it's just food. My prayer is that whoever decides to read my book may find a glimmer of hope and peace in whatever situation they find themselves in. If anyone is going through a difficult time in his or her life, and can glean anything from this book to help, it will give me a lot of joy. I'd like to pass on the growth I've experienced.

May you learn that all things may work together for good. I've been blessed: may you be as well!

Love, Mary

Afterward

Mary created these poems and drawings over thirty years ago. The calligraphy, poems and artwork are hers; the narrative is a result of a series of interviews she and I conducted in her home during the summer of 2012.

The Silver Lake Press logo was designed by Mary. Thank you!

For more information on personal histories, visit
www.marjorieturner.com

Marjorie Turner Hollman

Made in United States
North Haven, CT
10 November 2026

22096543R00065